HOW COMMUNITY GARDENS WORK

Louise Spilsbury

Gareth Stevens
Publishing

Please visit our website, www.garethstevens.com. For a free color catalog of all our high-quality books, call toll free 1-800-542-2595 or fax 1-877-542-2596.

Library of Congress Cataloging-in-Publication Data

Spilsbury, Louise.
How community gardens work / by Louise Spilsbury.
   p. cm. — (EcoWorks)
Includes index.
ISBN 978-1-4339-9557-6 (pbk.)
ISBN 978-1-4339-9558-3 (6-pack)
ISBN 978-1-4339-9556-9 (library binding)
1. Community gardens—Juvenile literature. 2. Organic gardening —Juvenile literature. I. Title.
SB457.3 S65 2014
635—dc23

First Edition

Published in 2014 by
Gareth Stevens Publishing
111 East 14th Street, Suite 349
New York, NY 10003

© 2014 Gareth Stevens Publishing

Produced by Calcium, www.calciumcreative.co.uk
Designed by Simon Borrough and Paul Myerscough
Edited by Sarah Eason and Ruth Bennett

Photo credits: Cover: Shutterstock: Laura Stone. Inside: Dreamstime: Alisonh29 2, 15, 24, Deniskelly 12, Jimsphotos 13, Jirikabele 18, Laozhang 9, Littleny 1, 6, Ltisha 14, Musat 21, Paha_l 27, Rainer 18, Rnonstx 4; Shutterstock: AISPIX by Image Source 23, Kasia Bialasiewicz 16, Elena Elisseeva 11, Iakov Filimonov 26, Goodluz 7, Nick Hawkes 25, D. Kucharski K. Kucharska 19, Lucy 29, nodff 28, Pinkcandy 22, Denis and Yulia Pogostins 10, Pressmaster 8, Jose Angel Astor Rocha 17, Laura Stone 5.

Printed in the United States of America

CPSIA compliance information: Batch #CS13GS: For further information contact Gareth Stevens,
New York, New York at 1-800-542-2595.

OCT - 2 2013

Contents

What Are Community Gardens?

Eagle Heights in Wisconsin is a very special garden. It has 1,000 gardeners tending it, who speak more than 60 languages between them. Eagle Heights is one of the United States' biggest and oldest community gardens. Community gardens are areas of land gardened by a group of people who don't have yards of their own.

Community Gardens in the Past

There have been community gardens in some form or another for as long as there have been cities. They provide a green space to escape crowds and grow food for families. They grew in number during the economic hardship of the 1930s and when food was short during and after World War II (1939–1945). During the war they were called "victory gardens," and there were more than 18 million in the United States alone!

Some community gardens are grown with everyone working together. Others are split into plots managed by different gardeners.

4

Community Gardens Today

The demand for community garden plots is increasing again today, especially in cities. The number of people living in towns and cities is rising fast and community gardens are important spaces where people can rest and play, or grow vegetables, fruits, flowers, and herbs. They range in size from small, low-cost neighborhood gardens to huge spaces divided into dozens of farm plots.

Many community gardens are important patches of green life for city dwellers.

ECO FACT

Positive Impact

The South Central community garden was opened in 1992 after devastating riots in Los Angeles, California. It was intended to create a sense of community in one of the city's most troubled neighborhoods and to feed struggling families. It covered 14 acres (5.6 ha) and contained 360 plots. Sadly, the garden closed in 2006, when the land was sold back to a previous owner. So many people fought to save it that the garden became famous and the story was even made into a film: *The Garden.*

Food for the People

Many community gardens are set up with the main aim of growing food. Growing your own food has many benefits. Just one is that it is often cheaper to grow your own produce than to buy it from stores, especially if you want to eat organic fruits and vegetables.

People of all ages can be involved in community gardens.

Healthy and Affordable

For many families living in cities, growing their own food is a reliable way of ensuring they get good-quality fresh fruits and vegetables. People on low incomes can grow nutritious foods that they would otherwise be unable to afford. Growing your own food also means you can grow varieties or types of produce that might not be available in the stores. Another benefit is that once people begin gardening, many find it satisfying to grow their own food.

ECO FACT

The Choices Are Endless

People grow a variety of foods in community gardens. They grow tomatoes, potatoes, and bell peppers, and even more exotic foods, such as bitter melon, snake gourds, and sesame leaves. In some gardens, people keep chickens for eggs and bees to make honey. In others, people grow ornamental fruit and vegetable plants, or grow flowers as well as food crops, so that these green spaces look good as well as provide great-tasting food.

Growing Organic

Organic food is grown using fewer chemicals such as pesticides. For example, rather than using chemical weed killers, organic farmers may spread manure to keep weeds at bay. Organic farming is time-consuming and some crops may not grow as well without artificial fertilizers to encourage growth. However, many people believe organic food tastes better and that less exposure to pesticides is better for your health.

Growing your own food means you can grow what you like in the way you like.

Rest and Recreation

As well as providing food, community gardens are a place for people to escape the noise and crowds of the city. People go to the gardens to rest, sunbathe, or watch birds and other wildlife. Families have picnics on the grass, sometimes with food they have grown themselves. Others go to walk their dogs or play sports. In some gardens, there are even performance areas for shows.

Community gardens give people a green space in which to rest and relax.

Gardens Are Good for You

Being in green spaces, whether playing games or just walking through a garden, soaking up the colors, sounds, and smells, reduces stress and increases a person's sense of well-being. Although people should take care to cover up in the sun, some sun is good for you—it helps the body to make vitamin D, which is essential for healthy bones.

Garden Yourself Fit!

When people have access to a community garden, they tend to be fitter, too. Gardening tasks that use leg, arm, shoulder, neck, back, and stomach muscles build strength and burn calories. Lifting bags and pots is as good as weightlifting, and all the bending and reaching involved in weeding and planting helps to make you more flexible.

It's healthy to have green spaces near buildings because plants help to clean our air.

Pollution Up Close

Plants make the air healthier! Burning fuels in cars and other vehicles release carbon dioxide and other pollutants into the air. Trees and other plants help to remove this air pollution. Plants clean our air by taking the carbon dioxide and converting it to oxygen. They also absorb dust, ash, and smoke through the pores (tiny holes) in the leaf surface.

Gardens for Learning

Many community gardens are built near schools, so that young people have a chance to experience gardening firsthand. Gardening is a great way to learn about nature, and it also teaches many other skills.

Real-Life Lessons

Community gardens teach people about where food comes from. They encourage healthy eating and an interest in cooking, as students learn to cook the foods that they grow and harvest. Working together on a garden teaches the importance of teamwork. Working out how much each plant produces improves math skills. Some schools sell produce that they grow in their garden, which teaches business skills that will be useful later in life. Gardening also teaches patience—it can take time for seeds to grow!

By caring for plants, people really understand what the plants need and how they grow.

Plant Care

To make a garden work, you need to know what plants need to grow. Plants need nutrients, which they take up through their roots from healthy soil. Soil also provides support for the plant and an anchor for the roots. Plants need light and water to make their food through a process called photosynthesis. Plants also need space to grow. If the space is small, the plants will be small.

Growing your own food gives you a real interest in cooking and eating it, too!

Garden Laboratories

School gardens are like living science laboratories. By measuring how plants grow under different conditions, students understand the effect of light, water, and different types of soil. Instead of reading about insects and other animals in a book, pupils can watch them in a garden to see what environments different creatures prefer. Instead of talking about how different plants might be grouped, or classified, students can see the differences in real life.

Sensory Gardens

Some community gardens are sensory gardens. Sensory gardens are designed to stimulate people's senses, so they can see, feel, taste, smell, and hear aspects of nature. Sensory gardens are often built close to facilities for children and adults who have mental or physical disabilities. Being outside can be especially beneficial for those who have to spend a large part of their lives indoors.

Accessible Nature

Sensory gardens are carefully laid out to be safe and easy to use. They usually have plenty of seats and gently sloping paths that are wide enough for wheelchairs. Sensory gardens often have raised flower beds, so that the plants are high enough for people to smell and feel easily. They also might have ponds and water features, and objects such as birdhouses and wildlife-friendly plants to attract birds, butterflies, and other animals.

Most people find the sounds of water and the smell of plants relaxing.

Pollination Up Close

Flowers produce scent to attract insects. Insects visit plants to feed on sweet liquid, called nectar, in the center of the flower. As they do so, pollen from the flower brushes onto their bodies. When the insects stop at other flowers, the pollen rubs off and helps that plant to reproduce and make more plants. This is called pollination.

Planting for the Senses

Plants are chosen to appeal to all the senses. Plants with colorful flowers or interesting leaves are enjoyable to look at. Plants, such as tall feathery grasses which swish together when a breeze blows, make interesting sounds to hear. Some flowering plants, such as rose and honeysuckle, release scents. People also plant scented herbs, such as rosemary and oregano, which are good to smell. Plants for touch include prickly holly, spongy moss, feathery fennel, and the soft leaves of plants such as coltsfoot.

Planting herbs in a sensory garden ensures the area will smell interesting and appealing.

13

Laying Out Gardens

The most important things to think about when planning a community garden are who it is for and when it will be used. Will the space provide flowers for a community or fruit and vegetables to feed many families? Will people use the garden all the time? For example, a school garden will be visited during the school year, but not during vacations.

Planning a Garden

Most community gardens are established on vacant or unused pieces of land. Communities buy or rent the land, or are granted use of it by the organization that owns it. Ideally it should be close to the people who will use it, on level ground so it is easier to work, and near a water source for people to water their plants.

A community garden works best if it is within walking distance of the people who will use it.

Some garden plots are divided into raised beds like these.

Garden Design

The layout of a community garden depends on whether it is going to be one big garden, or divided into plots. Plots are usually of equal sizes and are rented by individual gardeners. In shared community gardens, more planning is needed. Communities usually work together on sketches for an initial layout that might include ponds, an area for compost, sheds, benches, and a meeting area, as well as areas for growing flowers and produce, such as vegetables.

Crop Rotation Up Close

All vegetable gardens, big or small, should incorporate crop rotation into their plans. This is the practice of planting crops in a different plot each year. Crop rotation prevents diseases from building up in the soil, controls weeds by regularly changing their growing conditions, and prevents the soil from becoming worn out.

Garden Soil

Garden soil is made up of clay, sand, silt, and tiny pieces of organic matter, such as decaying leaves or animal waste. Gardens grow best when soil has a good balance of these materials. As community gardens are often built on wasteland, the soil may be not be healthy at first, and may need work to make it suitable for growing plants.

Mulching for Health

Once a community has removed large stones, debris, and waste from an area and dug out larger weeds, the land is often then covered with mulch. Mulch is a layer of material applied to the surface of an area of soil to improve it. Mulching prevents weeds from growing because it blocks out the light.

Biodegradable mulches improve soils when they break down by releasing nutrients into the soil. Common mulches include bark chips, straw, lawn cuttings, sawdust, newspapers, cardboard, leaf mold, seaweed, and old carpet.

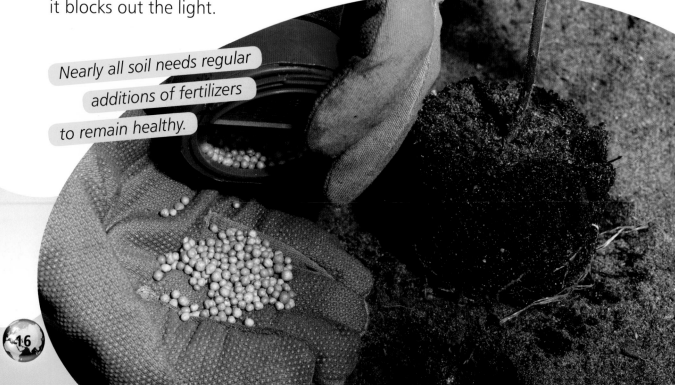

Nearly all soil needs regular additions of fertilizers to remain healthy.

Using Fertilizers

Gardeners also improve soil by adding manure or fertilizers to it. Fertilizers are nutrients that improve the number and the quality of crops you can grow in the soil. Many gardeners use green fertilizers, which are nutrient-rich plants, such as alfalfa and clover. They grow quickly and can be dug back in to the soil to give it valuable nutrients. Some gardeners also apply seaweed, which is rich in nutrients and minerals.

Many community gardens are developed on ground that looks worn out and useless.

Wasteland Up Close

Some wasteland is polluted by chemicals. Adding fertilizers to the soil provides nutrients that feed useful microorganisms, such as bacteria, which can clean up the harmful chemicals from polluted soil. This is called bioremediation.

- Microscopic living things, such as bacteria, live in soil and eat certain harmful chemicals.
- When microorganisms completely digest these chemicals, they change them into water and gases such as carbon dioxide.
- Microorganisms release the water and gases into the soil.

Composting

Composting is nature's way of recycling. All dead plants rot and decompose eventually, turning into a soil-like material called compost. Gardeners make compost heaps to help waste decompose faster. The compost makes an excellent natural fertilizer.

Many people start compost heaps in open wooden boxes like these.

Making a Compost Heap

To make a compost heap you need a space of around 10 square feet (1 sq m) and a container, such as a big old bin. Begin by spreading a "brown" layer of dry material, such as leaves, twigs, or old newspapers. Then put a "green layer" of waste, such as grass cuttings, food scraps, or coffee grounds. Repeat these layers when you have more waste to add. Every couple of weeks, add some water to keep the compost moist, and turn the pile over using a pitchfork. The compost is ready for use when the mixture turns dark and crumbly, looks like black soil, and smells sweet.

The Science of Composting

Compost can take several months to convert from the raw materials into the finished product. Animals, such as worms and pill bugs, crawl into the waste and help to break it down. They shred the waste into smaller pieces, creating a greater surface area for microorganisms such as bacteria and fungi. Microorganisms do most of the decomposition work in compost, eating and digesting the waste and turning it into heat, carbon dioxide, water, and compost.

Harmful Waste

Composting kitchen waste is an environmentally friendly thing to do. When vast amounts of food waste decompose in a landfill site, they produce methane, a greenhouse gas that contributes to global warming. In the United States alone, 23.5 million tons (21.3 million mt) of food is thrown away each year. Composting is a simple way to return food waste back to the earth and enrich the soil for the next harvest.

Compost in soil increases numbers of earthworms. This helps improve the soil because as they tunnel through soil, the earthworms mix it up, bringing in air and helping the soil to drain.

Pest Control

Garden pests are insects that damage plants. Some gardeners use chemical pesticides, which are powders or sprays that harm or kill the pests. However, the problem with pesticides is that they kill or damage useful insects, too. Many community gardeners try to use alternative ways of controlling garden pests.

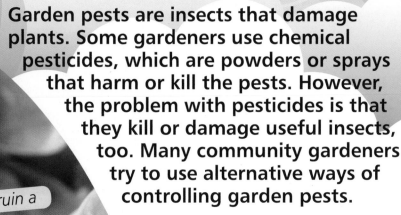

Pests, such as slugs, can ruin a gardener's plants.

Pest Attack

Some people cover their crops in netting. This stops butterflies from laying eggs, which hatch into hungry caterpillars that eat the plants. Another pest control method is to encourage wildlife into the garden, so that the wildlife will eat the pests. For example, if you grow plants such as sunflowers and ivy, which attract birds that feed on their seeds or berries, the birds will also eat insects. Slugs eat seedlings and plants. You can encourage ground beetles and toads into your garden by leaving pieces of wood for them to shelter under. The beetles and toads will return the favor by eating slugs, mites, and other pests in your garden!

Plant Power

Companion planting is growing particular plants close together in order to protect crops. For example, if you grow marigolds among your tomatoes, the marigolds release a strong smell that repels green flies and black flies, which can harm tomato plants. Gardeners often grow nasturtiums beside cabbages because caterpillars eat nasturtiums and leave the cabbages alone. If you put garlic plants among roses, the garlic will keep off aphids that can destroy the roses. Growing leeks and carrots together is smart, too. Leeks repel carrot flies and carrots repel onion flies and leek moths!

Young ladybugs are useful insects that eat aphid pests.

ECO FACT

Pesiticides Versus Bees

Some scientists think that pesticides are responsible for the dramatic decline in bee populations in the United States and other parts of the world. They say that pesticides affect the bees' brains so the insects cannot find their way back to their hives, and die. This is a serious problem because bees pollinate flowers, fruit, and other plants that we rely on. Without bees to help pollinate them, plants will begin to die out.

Watering the Plants

Plants need water. Water accounts for almost 95 percent of the body weight of a plant, and many smaller plants rely on water to stand upright—without it they wilt and droop. Plants use water to help them make their food by photosynthesis, and it also helps them to take in nutrients from the soil.

In summer, many plants need watering every day.

Saving Water

Water is a precious resource. Some places suffer from water shortages, especially in summer, so people must limit the amount of water they use. Many community gardens collect rainwater from roofs using gutters and troughs that channel the water into water containers.

Be Water Wise

Gardeners try to water their plants in the cool of the evening or early in the morning, rather than during the day, when most of the water would evaporate off the soil before reaching the plant roots. They also find ways to get the water directly to the roots of thirsty plants, such as by microdrip irrigation systems that drip water slowly into the ground so it soaks down to the roots, rather than running off or evaporating. Another method is to use a layer of mulch to retain moisture in the soil. Gardeners can also choose plants that will survive without watering!

Collecting rainwater in a water container like this saves gallons of tap water.

Transpiration Up Close

Plants take in water a bit like the way in which you suck water through a straw. Plants have tubes, called xylem, which run all the way from their roots to their leaves.

- Water escapes from little holes in the leaves when it is warmed. It evaporates, which means it turns into an invisible gas in the air called water vapor.
- When water evaporates from xylem in the leaves at the top of the plant, more water comes into the bottom of the tubes (in the roots) to replace it. This is called transpiration.

Growing Spaces

Many cities are short of land, but do have lots of unused, flat roofs. Urban gardeners often turn these into garden spaces. Growing plants improves air quality in cities and provides a habitat for butterflies, bees, and other wildlife.

Gardens can thrive on sunny rooftops.

Heating and Cooling

Gardens on roofs have an added benefit. Plants absorb heat and act as insulators for buildings, reducing the energy needed to provide heating. They also help to cool buildings. During the process of transpiration, water evaporates from their leaves, cooling the air. This means that people with roof gardens do not need to use air conditioning as often.

ECO FACT

Garden in the Sky

The roof garden on top of City Hall in Chicago, Illinois, has 20,000 plants, including 100 shrubs, 40 vines, and two trees. The plants are local to the area and were chosen because they are tough enough to cope with strong winds and little water. The soil they grow in is a special mix of compost, mulch, and sponge-like substances. It weighs less than regular soil and holds a lot more water.

This garden has a well-dressed scarecrow to keep hungry birds off the plants!

Making a Roof Garden

It takes a lot of effort to set up a roof garden. First, you have to lay a waterproof sheet to protect the building from leaks and act as a barrier to stop roots from growing through. There also needs to be a layer of gravel, clay, or felt that allows water to soak through, so it can be collected and used to water the plants. It's often windy on high roofs, so most roof gardens also have a wind barrier—this protects the plants and the gardeners! Plants are often grown in containers or in a shallow layer of soil.

Sharing Benefits and Responsibilities

Community gardens have many benefits, but they do take a lot of work. Community gardens need a group of people to run them, money to keep them going, rules for how they work, and enough people who believe in the project to keep it alive.

Responsibilities

Community gardens are often run by a management committee formed by local people, usually working on a voluntary basis (for no pay). To keep the gardens going, members of the community must take responsibility for the project, doing chores such as pruning, cleaning up litter, weeding, mowing lawns, and repairing the buildings.

Community gardens have many benefits but do require time and effort.

Raising Funds

The committee may organize fundraising events to help pay rent for the land. Community gardens might have short or temporary leases, so gardeners may have to campaign to ensure the garden is not taken over by developers.

Great Benefits

Communities get collective benefits from the gardens. They sell excess produce to stores or at farmers' markets. Some community gardens give produce to food charities. Community gardens make homes in the area desirable for buyers who value green spaces.

Working together means members of a community get to know each other and get along better together.

ECO FACT

Delivery!

Some community gardens deliver fresh fruits and vegetables, usually locally grown and often organic, either directly to the customer or to a local collection point. This allows community gardens to use their excess produce to raise funds to help keep their garden going.

Community Gardens in the Future

Many people today are concerned about using resources without harming the environment or our future resource supplies. They are interested in creating a sustainable way of life and avoiding things that harm our environment, such as food that is transported long distances and intensive farming. Choosing to be involved in a community garden is a way to tackle these issues, and it is becoming extremely popular.

Community gardens are good for people and for the environment.

Eat Local

Growing food in the city or among local communities relieves some pressure on farms. It reduces greenhouse gases and pollution released from fossil fuels used for food transport. Composting in community gardens reduces waste and therefore the amount of methane released from landfills. Smaller gardens are easier to farm organically and this reduces the amount of chemicals introduced into the earth. Community gardens also provide food and shelter for birds and insects.

On the Rise

As well as for environmental reasons, many people join a community garden for personal pleasure and to help keep their food costs down. In 1996, the American Community Gardening Association estimated that there were more than 6,000 community gardens in 38 US cities. Today there are more than 10,000! Government policy on these gardens is changing, too. At one time, community gardens were simply allowed to exist on unused land until a developer bought it. Today, local governments are establishing them as permanent sites. It looks like we will see many more community gardens in the future.

More and more people are getting involved in community gardens. Is there one near you?

ECO FACT

P-Patch Program

The Seattle P-Patch Program was formed in 1971 by a student who wanted more young people to learn how to grow vegetables. The "P" stands for "passionate people producing peas in public." Today it is the largest community gardening program managed by local government in the United States. It includes more than 60 gardens and around four new gardens are founded each year.

Glossary

bacteria microscopic living things found in air, water, soil, food, and even people. Some bacteria are useful. Others can cause disease.

biodegradable able to decompose, or break down, by a natural process

calories energy units in food

compost a mixture of decaying vegetation and manure that can be used as a fertilizer

crop rotation the process of moving crops around a plot each year to avoid pests and diseases, and to maintain good, fertile soil

decompose to decay or rot

evaporate to turn from a liquid into a gas

fertilizer a substance that is used to make soil more suitable for growing plants

fossil fuel fuels, such as coal, oil, and natural gas, which have formed from the remains of ancient plants and animals

global warming a rise in temperatures across the world, caused by polluting greenhouse gases in the air

greenhouse gas gases that make Earth warmer by absorbing some of the sun's heat

habitat a natural home for a group of plants and animals

insulators materials that do not allow heat to move through them easily

intensive farming a way of farming land in order to be able to grow as many crops on it as possible

landfill a site at which waste is buried under layers of soil

manure animal waste used to fertilize land

microorganism microscopic living thing

nutrient a matter that plants and animals need to grow and survive

organic farming a way of producing food without using chemical fertilizers and pesticides

pesticides chemicals used to kill pests that damage crops

photosynthesis a process by which green plants use sunlight to make food from carbon dioxide and water

pollen a powder-like substance produced by flowers that makes seeds develop

pollination the spreading of pollen between plants to make them produce seeds that grow into new plants

pollutants waste matter that contaminates the water, air, or soil

sustainable having to do with using resources without using them up or damaging the environment

transpiration a process by which plants release water through tiny pores in their leaves

For More Information

Books

Johnson, Daniel and Samantha. *The Beginner's Guide to Vegetable Gardening: Everything You Need to Know.* Minneapolis, MN: Voyageur Press, 2013.

Nagro, Anne. *Our Super Garden: Learning the Power of Healthy Eating, by Eating What We Grow.* Wilmette, IL: Dancing Rhinoceros Press, 2010.

Tornio, Stacy. *Project Garden: A Month-by-Month Guide to Planting, Growing, and Enjoying All Your Backyard Has to Offer.* Avon, MA: Adams Media, 2012.

Websites

Visit the American Community Gardening Association to find out how it supports all aspects of community food and ornamental gardening at: **www.communitygarden.org**

Discover how Green Guerillas provides services to community garden groups to help them care for their community gardens: **www.greenguerillas.org**

Find out how to start a community garden at: **tlc.howstuffworks.com/home/ community-garden.htm**

Index